When Tillie Rides Her Wheel

A whiz, a whir,
A dazzling blur,
    A flash of yellow hair,
A firm-set face,
A whirlwind pace,
    A wheel that splits the air!

Too slow our eyes—
So fast she flies
    Around the tilted curve
With wheel a-cant
At dizzy slant
    To catch her swooping swerve!

With swooping swerve—
How cool her nerve!—
    She swings into the lead;
She holds her place
In maddest race,
    As tireless as her steed!

The goal in sight—
How wild her flight,
    And how our senses reel
To see her rush
And hear the hush
    When Tillie rides her wheel!

Anonymous
Indianapolis Trade Journal
March 26, 1898

TILLIE

THE
TERRIBLE
SWEDE

How One Woman, a Sewing Needle, and a Bicycle Changed History

By Sue Stauffacher

Illustrated by Sarah McMenemy

Alfred A. Knopf · New York

For my niece Katie Hutchins, a perfect example of a
young woman who is both beautiful and strong.
And in memory of my Chicago-born Swedish grandmother,
Ruth Karin Hammer (née Erickson). —S.S.

For my mother, Gilia, with love. —S.M.

ACKNOWLEDGMENTS

I'd like to thank Alice Olson Roepke, who has been educating audiences about her grandmother's famous
bicycle-racing sister for more than ten years. Alice passionately shared her memories and Tillie's scrapbooks
and memorabilia with me. I also used several excellent publications from the nonprofit organization The
Wheelmen to find out more about the history of bicycling and Tillie Anderson. I am particularly grateful to
author Heather Drieth for her articles on Tillie.

For more information about Tillie Anderson, visit tillieanderson.com. Please visit The Wheelmen online
at thewheelmen.org. —S.S.

Library of Congress Cataloging-in-Publication Data
Stauffacher, Sue.
Tillie the terrible Swede : how one woman, a sewing needle, and a bicycle changed history /
by Sue Stauffacher ; illustrated by Sarah McMenemy. — 1st ed.
    p.   cm.
ISBN 978-0-375-84442-3 (trade) — ISBN 978-0-375-94442-0 (lib. bdg.)
1. Anderson, Tillie. 2. Cyclists—Sweden—Biography. 3. Cyclists—United States—Biography.
4. Women cyclists—Sweden—Biography. 5. Women cyclists—United States—Biography.
I. McMenemy, Sarah, ill. II. Title.
GV1051.A48S83 2009
796.62092—dc22
[B]
2010007083

The illustrations in this book were created using gouache paint, hand-painted paper collage, and black
india ink on Langton watercolor paper.

MANUFACTURED IN MALAYSIA
January 2011
10 9 8 7 6 5 4 3 2 1
First Edition

In the old days, most girls came to America with a dream, but all Tillie Anderson had was a needle. So she got herself a job in a tailor's shop and waited for a dream to come and find her. One fine day it rolled right by her window.

"Bicycles aren't for ladies," Tillie's mother reminded her. But Tillie wasn't listening. From that day on, she saved up her money and dreamed of nothing but riding. Not the slow and stately sort of riding. No, Tillie dreamed of the speedy, scorchy, racy kind of riding.

If Tillie insisted on a bicycle, her mother suggested that she ride like the other young ladies did, making slow, graceful figure eights or completing circles around a maypole. Above all, Tillie was not to be seen with "bicycle face."

But Tillie had other ideas. *I'm too weak to ride for long,* she thought. So every day after work, she pedaled for half an hour in the fresh air, lifted dumbbells, and swung Indian clubs over her head.

There was just one other problem. Tillie had found that riding in dresses and skirts meant spilling, not speeding, falling, not flying.

So . . .

Tillie used her noodle *and* her needle to make something entirely different from what was sold in the ladies' shop where she worked. When Tillie took off her coat for her next ride . . .

Her mother was horrified!

The neighbors were scandalized!

Tillie's friends were mortified!

(In fact, some of them stopped speaking to her.)

But Tillie was satisfied.

"They all think I'm wicked," Tillie told her new friend, a bicycle racer named Phillip Shoberg.

"Now you can enter a real race," Phillip said. "Some women do, you know."

So Tillie entered her first century race—that's one hundred miles!— and broke the women's record by eighteen minutes!

However, the real racing excitement happened on the velodrome. For six days, women raced an hour and a half in the afternoon and an hour and a half in the evening. Riding shoulder to shoulder with the other racers—with no protective gear or helmet—the woman who could stay on her bike and ride the farthest claimed the prize money.

"Now *that's* a competition," Tillie told Phillip.

At first, she had a little trouble staying upright on the tilted track. But once she got the hang of it, Tillie blew by all the other riders and set another new record.

In no time at all, Tillie was a whirling sensation! Poets wrote odes. Reporters begged her for interviews. Bicycle companies fought to get Tillie as their poster girl.

When Tillie
Rides Her Wheel

A whiz, a whir,
A dazzling blur,
A flash of yellow hair,
A firm-set face,
A whirlwind pace,
A wheel that splits the air!

Too slow our eyes—
So fast she flies
Around the tilted curve
With wheel a-cant
At dizzy slant
To catch her swooping
Swerve!

Indianapolis Trade Journal
March 26, 1898

JOL

TILLIE
GREA
FINISH

YOUNGSTO

THE

SHE
IS FAST
IE ANDERSON

The other riders weren't too keen on Tillie getting all the press. At a six-day race in Minneapolis, they decided to stop Tillie on the track. They bumped her bicycle. They punctured her tires—ten times!

Tillie tried to race on, but after the second day of pushing and punctures, she withdrew from the race while she could still stand.

Would this be the end of Tillie's lightning-fast career?

Not if Phillip could help it. Phillip had quit his racing career to become Tillie's manager. He paced her on rides. He cheered her on. He counted her push-ups.

Back in Chicago, Phillip encouraged Tillie to enter an even more difficult eighteen-hour race. Around and around the track, three hours a day for six days at dizzying speeds.

Even though everyone knew she was the fastest racer, the organizers put Tillie in a racing group with the slowest cyclists. Phillip was terribly upset. How would Tillie know how fast she needed to go to get a qualifying time? How would she pace herself?

"I'll just have to race against myself," Tillie told him. "I'm pretty darned fast."

By the end of the day, she was a mile ahead of the fastest racer in the fast heat. It seemed nothing could hold Tillie back. She won the race, set a new eighteen-hour record, and earned herself a nickname along with the prize money: Tillie the Terrible Swede.

Young girls on their bicycles thought Tillie was terrific. But not everyone did. The men in the Associated Cycling Clubs thought a woman racer was, well, unwomanly. "Too man-like and that is a great sin," they concluded.

A team of doctors asked to examine Tillie to see what the effects of strenuous exercise would be on a woman's body. Their results were published in the newspaper. "Although Miss Anderson's limbs are not as regular from an artistic point of view, her general health is better," the doctors reported. "Simply put, from head to foot, she is a mass of muscle." To prove it, they put a picture of Tillie's bare leg in the newspaper.

Her mother was horrified (she fainted).

Her friends were mortified (even the ones still talking to her).

But the ladies calling for women's rights were energized.

"Let me tell you what I think of bicycling," said Susan B. Anthony. "It has done more to emancipate women than anything else in the world. It gives a woman a feeling of freedom and self-reliance. I stand by and rejoice every time I see a woman ride by on a wheel."

Phillip knew Tillie was a mass of muscle, but he didn't have the same opinion that the doctors did.

He thought Tillie was a work of art.

"Maybe we should marry and make our partnership official," he suggested to Tillie.

Tillie thought it was a fine idea. And so, between races, that is just what they did.

Tillie raced on all through the 1890s, breaking her own records and becoming the undisputed women's bicycle-racing champion of the world.

But by the turn of the century, bicycle racing had given way to a whole new American pastime. Talk about speed! Tillie couldn't get enough of her new hobby . . .

... driving a motorcar!

START

Tillie's Record Breakers

1897
New half-mile record:
52 seconds!

1896
New eighteen-hour record:
359.6 miles!

1896
New century ride
(100-mile) record:
6 hours and 57 minutes!

1898
After a one-hour match
and a four-day race against
Lisette Martin of France,
Tillie is declared
Champion of the World!

1896
New six-hour
velodrome record:
**114 miles and
3,727$\frac{1}{17}$ feet!**